3/17   L6 5.5 .5 pt

The OREGON TRAIL

BY BENJAMIN PROUDFIT

Gareth Stevens
PUBLISHING

Please visit our website, www.garethstevens.com. For a free color catalog of all our high-quality books, call toll free 1-800-542-2595 or fax 1-877-542-2596.

Library of Congress Cataloging-in-Publication Data

Names: Proudfit, Benjamin, author.
Title: The Oregon Trail / Benjamin Proudfit.
Description: New York : Gareth Stevens Publishing, [2016] | Series: Road
  trip: famous routes | Includes index.
Identifiers: LCCN 2016006961 | ISBN 9781482446753 (pbk.) | ISBN 9781482449563 (library bound) | ISBN
9781482449457 (6 pack)
Subjects: LCSH: Oregon National Historic Trail–Juvenile literature. |
  Overland journeys to the Pacific–Juvenile literature. | Automobile
  travel–West (U.S.)–Juvenile literature. | West (U.S.)–Description and
  travel–Juvenile literature.
Classification: LCC F597 .P67 2016 | DDC 978–dc23
LC record available at http://lccn.loc.gov/2016006961

First Edition

Published in 2017 by
Gareth Stevens Publishing
111 East 14th Street, Suite 349
New York, NY 10003

Copyright © 2017 Gareth Stevens Publishing

Designer: Andrea Davison-Bartolotta
Editor: Kristen Nelson

Photo credits: Cover, p. 1 (left) Anton Foltin/Shutterstock.com; cover, p. 1 (right) Zack Frank/Shutterstock.com; p. 4 Joseph Sohm/Shutterstock.com; p. 5 zrfphoto/iStock/Thinkstock; p. 6 Malgorzata Litkowska/Shutterstock.com; pp. 7, 21 blinkblink/Shutterstock.com; p. 9 Posnov/Moment/Getty Images; p. 10 Danielle Pinc/Shutterstock.com; p. 11 Dan Thornberg/Shutterstock.com; p. 12 Gabe Rogel/Aurora/Getty Images; p. 13 Maxine Livingston/Shutterstock.com; p. 14 Deb G/Shutterstock.com; p. 15 (inset) Bourrichon/Wikimedia Commons; p. 15 (main) HES Photography/ Shutterstock.com; p. 16 John Elk/Lonely Planet Images/Getty Images; p. 17 B-A Graphix/Shutterstock.com; p. 18 somchaij/Shutterstock.com; p. 19 CrackerClips Stock Media/Shutterstock.com; p. 20 Bureau of Land Management/ Wikimedia Commons.

Printed in the United States of America

CPSIA compliance information: Batch #CS16GS: For further information contact Gareth Stevens, New York, New York at 1-800-542-2595.

Contents

Words in the glossary appear in **bold** type the first time they are used in the text.

Take the Trail!

Imagine your parents announced your family was moving across the country. You'd pack up all your favorite clothes and games. Now, imagine loading all your things into the back of a wagon and walking next to it for 3 to 4 months to reach your new home. That's what **pioneers** on the Oregon Trail did!

The Oregon Trail was one of the main **routes** west from the early 1840s into the 1860s. Today, it offers history, natural beauty, and fun for modern travelers!

Pit Stop

Pioneers traveled the Oregon Trail for many reasons, including to find gold in California and to get away from the **American Civil War** in the 1860s.

where found: between Independence, Missouri, and Oregon City, Oregon

year established: the first group to travel the whole length left in 1834; most used between 1840s and 1860s

length: about 2,000 miles (3,220 km)

number of travelers during peak years: 300,000 to 400,000

wildlife along the trail during the mid-1800s: bison, deer, bighorn sheep, ducks, rabbits

major attractions: wagon wheel ruts, the National Historic Oregon Trail Interpretive Center, Three Island Crossing State Park and other state and national parks, Fort Laramie

When on a road trip along the Oregon Trail, there's a lot to see and do!

Making History

During the 1800s, many people in the United States believed in **manifest destiny**. The Oregon Trail was one way settlers sought to make this dream a reality. By the 1860s, though, railroads crossed the growing United States. Fewer pioneers headed west by wagon.

In 1978, the US government wanted to make sure the route of the Oregon Trail was honored and remembered. It became a national historic trail mostly cared for by the National Park Service.

Devil's Gate, Wyoming

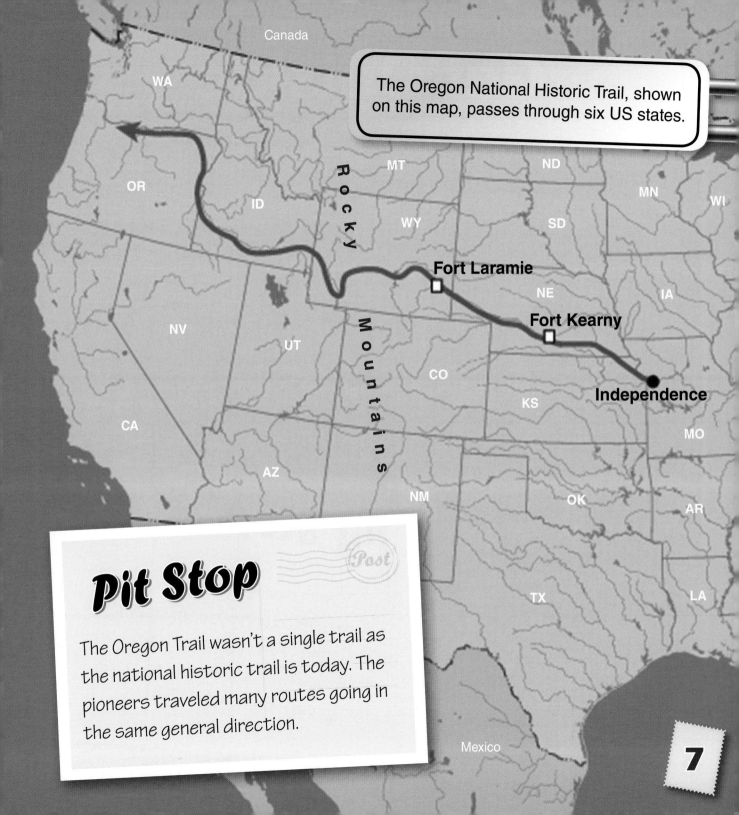

The Oregon National Historic Trail, shown on this map, passes through six US states.

Canada

WA
OR
ID
MT
ND
MN
WI
R o c k y
WY
SD
NE
IA
Fort Laramie
Fort Kearny
NV
UT
M o u n t a i n s
CO
Independence
CA
AZ
KS
MO
NM
OK
AR
TX
LA

Mexico

Pit Stop

Post

The Oregon Trail wasn't a single trail as the national historic trail is today. The pioneers traveled many routes going in the same general direction.

Get Outside

When on a road trip along the Oregon Trail, hiking is a must! However, visitors can't hike on all parts of the Oregon Trail, so it's important to read about the areas you want to hike ahead of time. That's because some of the trail passes through private land.

At Scotts **Bluff** National Monument in Gering, Nebraska, visitors can take a short hike to the **summit** of the bluff for beautiful views. The bluff was one of the most-mentioned landmarks written about in pioneer diaries.

Pit Stop

If you want to camp along the Oregon Trail, be sure to bring your own tent and supplies. Also, check with the park or town you want to camp in to make sure camping is allowed.

More than 250,000 pioneers passed Scotts Bluff on the Oregon Trail!

Auto Touring

The Oregon Trail is so long, it's likely you'll spend a lot of time in the car if you take a road trip along it. The National Park Service has mapped out a car route of roads and highways that follows the Oregon Trail as closely as it can!

Even driving along the Oregon Trail, travelers will see much of the same **geography** the pioneers did. From the grasslands of Kansas to the Blue Mountains, it's a **scenic** route. Be sure to take pictures!

Pit Stop

Post

The Oregon Trail is very close to several rivers, including the Snake, the Platte, and the Columbia Rivers. They provided pioneers with water to drink and wash with.

Platte River

The Columbia River flows through the Willamette Valley, where the Oregon Trail ends.

11

Many Parks

Nature lovers have many opportunities to visit national and state parks near the Oregon Trail. Biking, hiking, fishing, and wildlife watching are all activities visitors often take part in around the parks.

For more daring road trippers, a visit to the City of Rocks National **Reserve** can include rock climbing! Found near Burley, Idaho, it has tall rock formations some pioneers called a "city of tall **spires**." Nearby Castle Rocks State Park also offers camping and outdoor fun.

The pioneers heading west on the California Trail passed the rock spires now called City of Rocks National Reserve. The California Trail was a route to California that split from the Oregon Trail in southern Idaho.

13

Three Island Crossing

Crossing the Snake River was one of the hardest parts of the Oregon Trail journey. If the water was too high, pioneers headed south to cross. This took them through a dry, hot desert.

When the water was low enough, they could cross the river and take the easier route to the north. Today, Three Island Crossing State Park in Idaho is found where some pioneers would cross the Snake River! Visitors can learn more about the crossings in the museum and on the trails there.

Pit Stop

Some visitors ride horses along the Oregon Trail, just like the pioneers did! There are special places along the trail that allow easy entry for those riding horses.

Snake River is the largest **tributary** of the Columbia River.

Columbia River

Canada

WA

MT

ID

OR

Snake River

WY

CA

NV

UT

Living History

Many places important to the pioneers can still be seen today! Fort Laramie was established in 1834 as a fur trading post. It was also one of the places pioneers stopped on their way to the West, often to gather more supplies or rest.

The Fort Laramie National Historic Site is a great place to learn about **frontier** living during the 1800s. Visitors can tour the historic buildings and meet people dressed like those who spent time there!

Pit Stop

You can still see deep wagon wheel ruts in a part of the trail nearly all Oregon Trail travelers crossed at Oregon Trail Ruts National Historic Landmark near Guernsey, Wyoming!

Fort Laramie was a place pioneers on the Oregon Trail could feel safe.

Trail to Cities

Not everyone traveling the Oregon Trail was headed to Oregon. But the end of the Oregon Trail did lead to the growth of cities in that area.

Portland, Oregon, is less than an hour from Oregon City, where the trail ended. Founded in 1843, Portland is a growing city that's known for many parks and its citizens' love of the outdoors. Nearby, Mount Hood stands 11,239 feet (3,426 m) tall. It's a popular place for visitors to enjoy skiing, hiking, camping, and climbing.

Mount Hood

Portland is found where the Willamette River meets the Columbia River. River cruises are fun ways to see the city and the beauty around it!

Visit and Learn

You'll learn a lot by taking a road trip along the Oregon Trail—even if you aren't traveling by wagon! Many towns and parks on the route have museums that tell about the history of the trail.

One of the best of these is the National Historic Oregon Trail Interpretive Center near Baker City, Oregon. It has a 13-mile (21 km) section of wagon wheel ruts as well as artwork about the Oregon Trail and **replica** wagons. What a great way to end a road trip!

Pit Stop

Post

For the 150th anniversary of the Oregon Trail in 1993, many people reenacted traveling the route, including dressing and eating like the pioneers.

More Cool Stops Along the
Oregon Trail

Whitman Mission
Walla Walla, Washington

Learn about the settlers and the nearby Native Americans they met.

Fort Caspar
Casper, Wyoming

This frontier house has a museum and a bridge over the Platte River.

Devil's Gate
Natrona County, Wyoming

Over time, Sweetwater River has worn away rock to create this awesome natural landmark.

Soda Springs
Soda Springs, Idaho

The water here naturally has bubbles, like a soda!

Glossary

American Civil War: a war fought from 1861 to 1865 in the United States between the Union (the Northern states) and the Confederacy (the Southern states)

bluff: a high, steep bank beside a river or plain

frontier: a part of a country that has been newly opened for settlement

geography: the features of an area

manifest destiny: the belief that the United States should spread all the way to the Pacific Ocean

pioneer: one of the first American settlers to travel to and settle in the West

replica: a copy

reserve: land set aside for wildlife

route: a path people travel

scenic: having to do with the beauty of the natural landscape

spire: a cone-shaped pile or mass

summit: the top of a mountain

tributary: a river that joins a larger river or a lake

For More Information

Books

Freedman, Jeri. *Life as a Pioneer on the Oregon Trail.* New York, NY: Cavendish Square Publishing, 2016.

Hengel, Katherine. *Cool Parks & Trails: Great Things to Do in the Great Outdoors.* Minneapolis, MN: ABDO Publishing, 2016.

Ziff, John. *Northwest: Idaho, Oregon, Washington.* Broomall, PA: Mason Crest, 2015.

Websites

Kids in Parks
nps.gov/kids/index.cfm
Learn about ways you can enjoy the national parks and trails all over the United States.

Westward Expansion: Oregon Trail
ducksters.com/history/westward_expansion/oregon_trail.php
Find out more about the Oregon Trail and the pioneers who traveled it.

Index